THE BOOK OF
CRAFTS

Memoria Press
Classical Core Curriculum

Kindergarten

Tara Luse

MEMORIA PRESS
www.MemoriaPress.com

THE BOOK OF CRAFTS
Memoria Press Classical Core Curriculum

KINDERGARTEN
Tara Luse

ISBN #978-1-61538-477-8

First Edition © 2013 Memoria Press

Illustrated by Jessica Osborne, Starr Steinbach, & Karah Force

CONTENTS

CRAFT BOOK
Supply List

- ☐ Acrylic paints (blue, purple, and yellow)
- ☐ Apples
- ☐ Art pastels (yellows, browns, greens)
- ☐ Baking pan (disposable, 9" x 13" with lip)
- ☐ Bird seed
- ☐ Bowl
- ☐ Brads or paper fasteners
- ☐ Brown paper bag
- ☐ Cardstock (white, green, blue, and 1 other color)
- ☐ Cinnamon
- ☐ Clothes pins
- ☐ Colored pencils
- ☐ Construction paper (basic colors)
- ☐ Cotton swabs
- ☐ Crayons
- ☐ Cream of tartar
- ☐ Cupcake liners (regular and mini)
- ☐ Dirt
- ☐ Flour
- ☐ Flowers
- ☐ Foam paintbrush
- ☐ Fork
- ☐ Glitter
- ☐ Glue (white, liquid, stick)
- ☐ Googly eyes
- ☐ Gravel

- ☐ Greenery
- ☐ Grocery store circulars
- ☐ Hand-held mirror
- ☐ Hole punch
- ☐ Knife
- ☐ Magnifying glass
- ☐ Marbles
- ☐ Markers
- ☐ Newspaper
- ☐ Notecards
- ☐ Old toothbrush
- ☐ Paint (orange, green, yellow, brown, white, red, blue, purple)
- ☐ Paintbrush
- ☐ Paper plates (sturdy)
- ☐ Paper towels
- ☐ Pencil sharpener
- ☐ Pine boughs (freshly cut, small)
- ☐ Pipe cleaners (green)
- ☐ Plastic lid (large)
- ☐ Popsicle sticks
- ☐ Pruning shears
- ☐ Ribbon (red)
- ☐ Rock (1 small, round)
- ☐ Ruler (plastic)
- ☐ Salt (small grain, large grain, coarse)
- ☐ Sand
- ☐ Saucepan
- ☐ Scissors
- ☐ Shaving cream

- ☐ Solid shortening
- ☐ Spoon
- ☐ Spray bottle
- ☐ Stapler
- ☐ Straws
- ☐ Tape (clear, masking)
- ☐ Thread (white)
- ☐ Tissue paper (red, yellow, blue, light and dark green)
- ☐ Toilet paper rolls
- ☐ Toothpicks
- ☐ Twigs
- ☐ Twine, feathers, sequins, buttons, etc. (for decorating)
- ☐ Vegetable oil
- ☐ Vellum paper sheets
- ☐ Votive candle holder (clear)
- ☐ Water
- ☐ Watercolor paper
- ☐ Watercolors
- ☐ Wax paper
- ☐ White fabric (optional)
- ☐ White paper (8.5" x 11" and 11" x 14")
- ☐ Wood pencil
- ☐ Wooden craft sticks (jumbo)
- ☐ X-Acto knife
- ☐ Yarn (orange, purple, dark green)

INTRODUCTION

The creative arts are an essential part of the primary school education. By using the activities in this book, you can reinforce number and letter recognition, strengthen fine-motor skills, and foster creativity and confidence.

This book is for the youngest crafters and is intended to be a supplement to the Kindergarten curriculum. For easy reference, the crafts are separated into two categories: Literature Crafts and Concept Crafts.

The best way to work through these craft activities is to begin with reading all directions thoroughly and assembling any supplies you will need to complete the project. Please note that some activities require adult help, and several of the crafts contain small items.

While the crafts in this book have been carefully chosen to promote skill growth and coordination, the most important component is fun. Enjoy each of your creations and the time spent with your child making them!

LITERATURE CRAFTS

A TREE IS NICE
Tree Made From Tissue Paper

Supplies:

- [ ] tree template copied onto blue cardstock
- [ ] brown construction paper
- [ ] tissue paper squares cut to 1 inch – light green
- [ ] tissue paper squares cut to 1 inch – dark green
- [ ] white glue
- [ ] wood pencil

Teacher Guidelines:

1. Using the tree template as a guide, tear thin strips of the brown construction paper and glue them onto the trunk portion of the template. Cover the trunk shape completely, overlapping the brown paper edges to form the "bark" of the tree. When the tree trunk is completely covered, set it aside to dry.

2. When the tree is dry, spread a small area of the tree's branches section with glue. Be sure to cover only a small section with glue at a time, so the glue will not dry while twisting the tissue paper leaves.

3. Take one square of the tissue paper and place it in the palm of your hand. With the other hand, gently press the eraser end of the pencil into the center of the tissue square and close your fist around the paper and eraser. This will smash the tissue paper around the eraser tip of the pencil. Gently move the tissue paper on the eraser to the glued section of the tree and stick the tissue paper into the glue. The paper should slip easily off the end of the pencil. Continue using the tissue squares to cover the top of the tree, alternating between different shades of green until the tree's top is covered.

HOW TO MAKE AN APPLE PIE
AND SEE THE WORLD
Making a Passport

Supplies:

- ☐ passport cover template copied onto blue cardstock
- ☐ passport pages template copied onto white paper
- ☐ pencil
- ☐ small picture of the child
- ☐ glue
- ☐ stapler

Teacher Guidelines:

1. Begin by cutting out the blue passport cover. Fold in half along line. Set aside.
2. Using the pencil, have the child write their name in the space provided.
3. Glue the small picture into the box provided.
4. Cut white passport pages apart on the dotted lines.
5. To assemble the passport, stack the white pages, face up, in the following order:
   - Name page & Home (bottom)
   - Italy & Vermont, USA
   - France & Jamaica
   - Sri Lanka & England (top)
6. Place the white pages into the passport cover, and staple to secure.

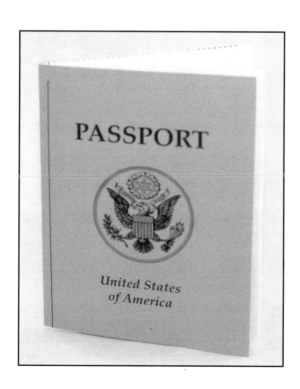

HUBERT'S HAIR RAISING ADVENTURE
Lion With Yarn Hair

Supplies:

- [ ] 1 lion head template printed onto cardstock
- [ ] crayons
- [ ] white, liquid glue
- [ ] orange yarn
- [ ] kid-safe scissors

Teacher Guidelines:

1. Cut the lion head template from the cardstock along the dotted line square around the outside.
2. Use the crayons to color the lion's face and ears.
3. Have an adult hold several lengths of the orange yarn together in a rope, allowing the child to cut small (1-2") sections with the safety scissors. Repeat until you have several large piles of cut yarn for "hair."
4. Spread a thick layer of liquid white glue on the space between the colored section of the template (the face) and the edge of the square. Do not put glue on the colored face section.
5. Let the child drop sections of cut yarn onto the glue-covered surface. Repeat until the glued area is covered in yarn. You may need to keep yarn from straying too close to the lion's face.
6. Allow the yarn to dry completely.
7. Have the child use the safety scissors to trim any over-hanging yarn from the edges of the outside of the square and around the face.

THE IMPORTANT BOOK
An All-About-Me Craft

Supplies:

- ☐ 1 fold book template
- ☐ crayons
- ☐ pencil
- ☐ X-Acto knife

Teacher Guidelines:

1. Decorate the front cover of the book (My Important Book panel). Instruct the child to write their name on the name box's line. Now, together, work through each color box, letting the child/children talk about their favorite things that coincide with each color: blue, red, yellow, and green. The child can either write the words of the things they choose for each color, or they can draw small pictures. On the last page, talk to the child and let them decide on what they think is most important about them. Write a few words in the space provided.

2. To Fold the Book:
   Fold the paper in half (along the center line) down the long side of the paper. Unfold it. Fold the paper in half (along the center line) down the short side of the paper. Unfold it. Place the paper horizontally on the table, so that the long sides are on the top and bottom. Take the left (short side) and fold it in towards the middle, vertical fold. Crease it well and unfold. Take the right side of the paper (short side) and fold it towards the middle of the page's vertical fold. Crease well and unfold. Now, having an adult use the X-Acto knife, cut along the line between the arrows.

3. After cutting between the arrows, fold along the long center line, so that the cut line is on the top. Grasp each short side of the folded paper and push them towards each other. Position the front and back covers and give it one final crease.

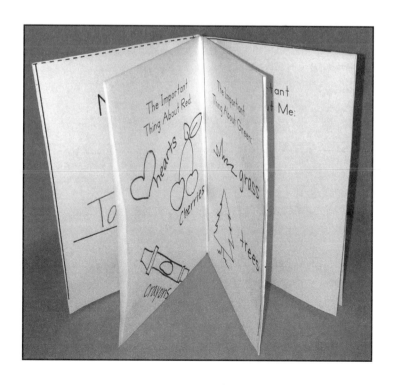

FREDERICK
Primary Color Sun Catchers

Supplies:

- ☐ large plastic lid (deli containers, whipped topping containers, etc.)
- ☐ liquid glue
- ☐ paintbrush
- ☐ tissue paper squares (1 inch): red, yellow, and blue
- ☐ small knife (for adult use only)
- ☐ white thread

Teacher Guidelines:

1. Working in a small section at a time, spread a thin layer of liquid glue onto the plastic lid with the paintbrush. While the glue is still wet, layer the tissue paper squares on top of the wet glue, overlapping slightly so the primary colors blend with each other. Continue gluing the tissue paper until the lid is fully covered. Set aside to dry.
2. When the lid is completely dry, have an adult poke a small hole in the lid with the knife and tie a length of thread through the hole. Hang up in a sunny spot.

FOLLOW THE DREAM
Boat Building

Supplies:

- ☐ 1 sheet of brown construction paper
- ☐ scissors
- ☐ hole punch
- ☐ 2 brads or paper fasteners
- ☐ 2 straws

- ☐ scissors
- ☐ clear tape
- ☐ 2 (3″ x 3″) squares of white paper
- ☐ 2 (2″ x 2″) squares of white paper

Teacher Guidelines:

1. To begin, cut the construction paper into 9 (1 inch wide by 12 inches long) strips. Trim strips to 6 inches in length.
2. Using the hole punch, punch holes on both ends of the paper strips, about a ½ inch from the edge and trying to keep the holes uniform through each of the strips.
3. Stack the strips on top of each other and slide a brad/fastener into the holes and open the backs to secure the stack together. Gently slide the strips apart, forming the bottom of the boat. Arrange the strips so that they overlap slightly and form a bowl shape. Set aside.
4. On one end of each of the straws, use the scissors to cut a ½ inch slit on opposite sides of each other. Set aside.
5. Next, punch a hole in the center of the top side of each of the squares. Punch another hole in each square in the center of the bottom of the square. Each square should have two holes, opposite each other. Take the larger square and slide the bottom hole onto the straw first. As you move the square down the straw, slide the top hole onto the straw as well. This will form the bottom, larger sail of the boat. Move the square down the straw until it is in the center of the straw. Repeat on the second straw with the other larger square of paper.
6. Next, add the smaller white square of paper to the tops of the straws in the same way. Finally, open the cut bottom of the straws, forming two flaps. Secure the flaps with tape to the bottom of the boat.

OX-CART MAN
Paper Weaving

Supplies:

- [ ] 1 sheet 9″ x 12″ brown construction paper
- [ ] ruler
- [ ] pencil
- [ ] scissors
- [ ] 1 sheet yellow construction paper
- [ ] 1 sheet orange construction paper
- [ ] clear tape

Teacher Guidelines:

1. First, an adult should use the ruler to mark off the weaving area on the brown sheet of construction paper. As the paper lays horizontally on the table, mark a 1/2 inch in on each of the long sides of the paper. Mark in 1 inch on each of the short sides of the paper. This will be your weaving area. Fold the paper in half, so that it measures 4.5 inches x 12 inches. Make a small pencil mark on the fold, every 2 inches.
2. Using scissors, cut from the mark on the fold to the line you drew earlier. Open the paper up, and you have your weaving mat.
3. To make the strips to weave with, cut the yellow and orange construction paper into 2 x 12 strips.
4. Now you can begin to weave. Start at the beginning of each row and move the strip through the mat—over, under, over, under—until you reach the end of the mat. An adult may have to help the child push the strips close together. Use a bit of tape on the ends to hold the strips in place.

PUMPKIN MOONSHINE
Paper Bag Pumpkins

Supplies:

- [ ] brown paper bag – lunch size
- [ ] black crayon
- [ ] newspaper
- [ ] paintbrush
- [ ] orange paint
- [ ] green paint

Teacher Guidelines:

1. To begin, lay the bag flat on the table and have the child use the black crayon to draw on the pumpkin's face on the lower half of the bag.
2. Open the bag up. Crumple up the newspaper into loose balls and stuff it into the bag. When the bag is about 2/3 full, begin twisting the top 1/3 of the bag. Keep twisting the top of the bag until it resembles a pumpkin's stem. Shape the filled bag into the desired pumpkin shape.
3. Using the paintbrush, paint the bottom of the bag orange and the top of the bag green.

THE STORY OF FERDINAND
Tissue Paper Flowers

Supplies:

- [ ] colored tissue paper
- [ ] ruler
- [ ] pencil
- [ ] scissors
- [ ] pipe cleaner

Teacher Guidelines:

1. Layer several sheets of tissue paper together.
2. Lightly mark a 6" x 6" square. Use the scissors to cut out the square.
3. Next, begin at one side of the square and do a 1-inch accordion fold until you reach the opposite side. (The accordion fold involves folding the paper 1 inch in one way, then flipping the square and folding it one inch in the other direction).
4. When the entire square is folded, wrap one end of the pipe cleaner around the center of the tissue paper and secure it by twisting. Gently separate each layer of tissue paper by pulling upwards toward the middle of the flower. Continue until both sides have been separated and pulled up.

PANCAKES, PANCAKES!
Cutting and Pasting Recipe Craft

Supplies:

☐ pancake plate template   ☐ scissors

☐ several grocery store circulars   ☐ glue stick

☐ crayons

Instructions:

1. Begin by letting the child color the pancake plate template with crayons. Next, look through the grocery store circulars to find the following pancake recipe ingredients:
    *   flour   *   butter
    *   eggs   *   sugar
    *   milk

2. Cut out examples of the recipe ingredients. Using the glue, stick the recipe ingredients onto the plate of pancakes.

BREAD AND JAM FOR FRANCIS
Yarn Craft

Supplies:

- ☐ toast pieces template
- ☐ crayons
- ☐ white glue
- ☐ purple yarn

Teacher Guidelines:

1. Use the crayons to color the outside part of the bread (leaving the center shape white).
2. After coloring, spread a thin layer of white glue onto the center space on the bread.
3. Beginning in the corner, glue the yarn from side to side until you reach the opposite corner. Press the yarn into the glue firmly.

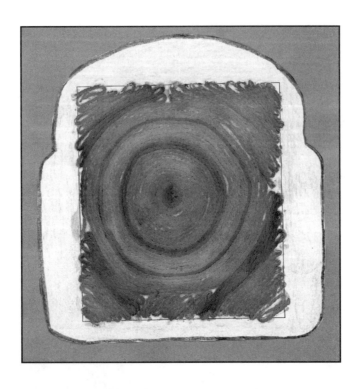

THE FIRST THANKSGIVING
Napkin Rings

Supplies:

- ☐ 2 cardboard toilet paper rolls
- ☐ scissors
- ☐ glue
- ☐ twine, feathers, markers, sequins, buttons, etc., for decorating

Teacher Guidelines:

1. Cut toilet paper rolls into 2-inch sections using the scissors.
2. When the rolls have been cut, color with markers and/or decorate with bits of twine, feathers, buttons, etc.
3. Use by folding napkins into a rectangle and feeding the long ends through the toilet paper tube.

THE LITTLE FIR TREE
Pine Wreath

Supplies:

- [ ] sturdy paper plate with the center cut out
- [ ] scissors
- [ ] paintbrush
- [ ] green paint
- [ ] pruning shears
- [ ] freshly cut (small) pine boughs
- [ ] dark green yarn
- [ ] red ribbon

Teacher Guidelines:

1. To begin, have an adult use the scissors to cut out the center of the paper plate, leaving only the outer 1.5 inches of the plate. Discard center circle.
2. Allow the child to use the paintbrush to paint the entire plate circle green. Set aside to dry.
3. While the plate is drying, use the pruning shears to cut 10-15 small (3-4 inch) sections of fresh pine branches. When the wreath base is dry, begin to add the pine boughs, one small section at a time. Holding the wreath, lay one pine branch on the ring (so the branch section sits completely inside the ring) and use the dark green yarn to wrap a section of the branch that sits between a small fork in the wood, and wrap around the plate. This will help the boughs sit securely on the ring.
4. Add the next pine section, so that the needle end overlaps the yarn area from the previous bough, covering it completely. Continue, adding pine sections until the entire plate ring is covered.
5. Use red ribbon to hang.

THE TWELVE DAYS OF CHRISTMAS
Creating an Advent Calendar

Supplies:

- ☐ advent calendar numbers template
- ☐ red crayon
- ☐ scissors
- ☐ glue
- ☐ 25 cardstock rectangles, 2" x 3"

- ☐ 25 clothespins
- ☐ red ribbon or yarn – approx. 10 feet
- ☐ 25 items to clip to the numbers (bible verses, candies, stickers, or small treats)

Teacher Guidelines:

1. The first step in making the calendar is to have the child trace the numbers on the template in crayon. After each number traced, have the child use the scissors to cut along the template's dotted lines, separating the numbers. Glue each number to a separate rectangle, centering it in the rectangle.
2. To assemble the calendar, clip each small treat or verse to the back of the rectangle with the number on it and clip it to the ribbon in number order, about 1 inch apart.
3. Hang the ribbon (with the clothespins/rectangles) somewhere in your home (i.e., fireplace mantle, bookshelf, etc.).
4. The child should unclip one numbered rectangle daily, corresponding to the day of December.

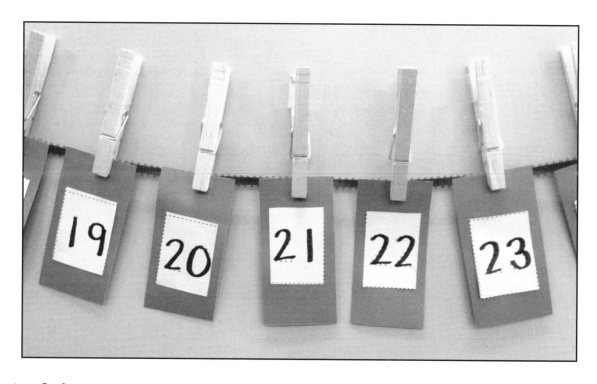

MR. WILLOWBY'S CHRISTMAS TREE
Handprint Christmas Tree

Supplies:

- [ ] 11" x 14" piece of white paper
- [ ] green paint
- [ ] yellow paint
- [ ] brown paint
- [ ] paintbrush

Teacher Guidelines:

1. Begin by laying out the large piece of white paper.
2. Paint one of the child's hands with the green paint and gently lay it in the center of the top of the paper, about 2 inches down from the top. The fingers of the hand should face away from the top edge of the paper.
3. Next, apply more paint and begin the second row of handprints. This row should have two prints in it. Continue with three or four prints in the third row. When all three rows are complete, use the paintbrush to paint a yellow start at the top of the tree, and a brown trunk at the bottom. Set aside to dry.

STELLALUNA
Constructing a Fruit Bat

Supplies:

- [ ] fruit bat template
- [ ] light brown crayon
- [ ] scissors

- [ ] hole punch
- [ ] 2 brads / paper fasteners

Teacher Guidelines:

1. Using the brown crayon, color the bat template (both the body and the wings).
2. Using the scissors, carefully cut out all three sections of the bat.
3. When the bat is cut out, color the other sides of the body and wings.
4. In the indicated circles on the wings and the sides of the body, use the hole punch to make small circles. Using the brads or paper fasteners, slip the brads into the front of the holes, through the wings and then the body. Open up the back of the brad to secure, leaving a little wiggle room so that the wings can move freely.

OWL MOON
Creating Owls From Toilet Paper Rolls

Supplies:

- ☐ toilet paper rolls
- ☐ washable acrylic paint (any colors)
- ☐ paintbrushes
- ☐ construction paper in orange and any other colors for decoration
- ☐ scissors
- ☐ glue
- ☐ googly eyes

Teacher Guidelines:

1. To begin, fold half of the toilet paper roll down towards the center of the tube (about 1 inch in size). Fold the other side of the top down exactly the same way. Now, use the paint and paintbrush to cover the toilet paper roll completely with paint. Set aside to dry.
2. When the toilet paper roll is completely dry, cut a 1-inch triangle from orange paper for the owl's beak and glue it about an inch down from the top of folded roll, pointing down. Next, glue on the googly eyes just above the beak.
3. Paint the owl's breast as pictured. Set aside to dry.
4. Lastly, from any color construction paper, cut two 2-inch ovals (with drawn feathers) and glue them to the sides of the paper roll. Let dry completely.

STOPPING BY WOODS
ON A SNOWY EVENING
Crayon Resist

Supplies:

- ☐ white heavy-weight cardstock or watercolor paper
- ☐ white crayon
- ☐ watercolor paint in very light blue and very light green
- ☐ paintbrush
- ☐ bowl filled with water

Teacher Guidelines:

1. Using the white crayon, draw a horizon line on the white paper. From the horizon line down, use the crayon to color in the snowy bottom of the forest. From the horizon line up, draw pine trees, bushes, etc.

2. When you have used your white crayon to add the snowy details to the picture, use the blue watercolor paint to paint the area above the horizon line. Rinse your brush, and use the green paint to paint the area below the horizon line. Set aside to dry.

GREGORY'S SHADOW
Shadow Printing

Supplies:

☐ dark-colored construction paper

☐ natural objects – leaves, twigs, flowers, small branches, shells

☐ a sunny day

Teacher Guidelines:

1. Begin by collecting natural objects from your surroundings.
2. Place your piece of construction paper in a very sunny spot, where it will not be disturbed. Place your items on the sheet and let it sit in the sun for 2 to 3 hours.
3. When the time is up, remove the items from the paper and enjoy the shadows left behind.

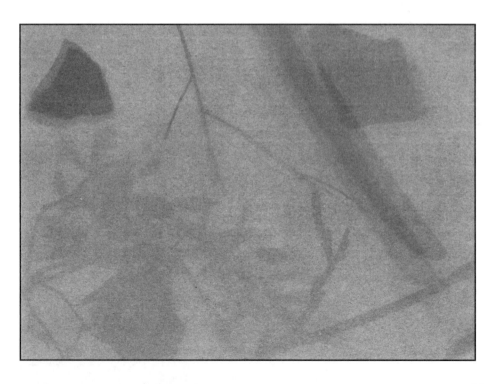

KATY AND THE BIG SNOW
Marble Painting

Supplies:

☐ house scene template copied onto blue 8.5" x 11" cardstock

☐ masking tape

☐ disposable 9" x 13" inch baking pan with lip

☐ white paint

☐ 3 marbles

Teacher Guidelines:

1. Using the tape, secure the blue cardstock (with the copied template on it) to the bottom of the baking pan.

2. Squirt a nickel-sized glob of white paint onto the baking pan at either end, just outside the paper's edge. Drop in the marbles. Allow the child to lift the pan and shift it from side to side, letting the marbles roll through the paint and across the picture. Keep shifting the pan until the page is covered with white painted "snow" tracks.

3. Set aside to dry.

WALTER THE BAKER
Homemade Cinnamon Salt Dough

Supplies:

☐ 1 cup water

☐ 1 tablespoon vegetable oil

☐ 1/2 cup salt

☐ 1 tablespoon cream of tartar

☐ 1 cup flour

☐ 1 t. ground cinnamon

☐ saucepan

Teacher Guidelines:

1. Combine water, oil, salt, and cream of tartar in a saucepan and heat until warmed through.
2. Remove from heat, adding flour and cinnamon.
3. Stir vigorously until combined. Remove from saucepan and knead until smooth and cooled completely.
4. Store this dough in an airtight container for up to 3 months.

THE FROGS AND TOADS ALL SANG
Painted Rocks

Supplies:

- [ ] 1 small round rock
- [ ] water and paper towels
- [ ] frog legs template
- [ ] green cardstock
- [ ] scissors

- [ ] green paint
- [ ] white paint
- [ ] paintbrush
- [ ] liquid glue
- [ ] 2 googly eyes

Teacher Guidelines:

1. Wash your rock thoroughly and set it aside to dry on the paper towels. While the rock is drying, copy the frog legs template onto the green cardstock. Use the scissors to cut the legs out and set them aside.

2. When the rock is dry, paint it entirely with the green paint. Set aside to dry. When the green paint is dry, use the white paint to make spots onto the frog. When the white paint is dry to the touch, glue the googly eyes to the top (near the end). Set aside to dry.

3. When the frog is dry, use the glue to fasten the cardstock legs to the bottom of the rock, and let dry.

ROXABOXEN
Natural Diorama

Supplies:

☐ paper plate

☐ brown paint

☐ paintbrush

☐ sand

☐ dirt

☐ small gravel stones

☐ twigs

☐ little bits of greenery

☐ 4 popsicle sticks (cut in half)

☐ liquid glue

Teacher Guidelines:

1. Cover the paper plate with a thick layer of brown paint, using the paintbrush. While the paint is still wet, sprinkle it with sand and dirt. Set aside to dry.

2. When the sand/paint mixture is dry, arrange your Roxaboxen hill with bits of gravel, twigs, greenery, and broken popsicle-stick boxes. Use the liquid glue to secure. Let dry completely.

CACTUS HOTEL
Sandpaper Cactus

Supplies:

- [ ] cactus scene template copied onto white paper
- [ ] crayons
- [ ] ¼ c. sand
- [ ] ¼ c. green paint
- [ ] bowl and spoon

Teacher Guidelines:

1. Use the crayons to color the cactus scene, leaving the cactus blank.
2. In a mixing bowl, combine the sand and green paint with the spoon.
3. Using your fingers, spread a thick layer of the green sand paint onto the cactus outline. Set aside to dry.

HIDE AND SEEK FOG
Making a Foggy Scene

Supplies:

☐ lighthouse template

☐ white watercolor paper

☐ watercolor paints

☐ watercolor paintbrush

☐ vellum paper sheets

☐ stapler

Teacher Guidelines:

1. Transfer the lighthouse template onto watercolor paper. Let the child use the watercolor paints and brush to paint the entire scene. Set aside to dry.
2. When the paint is dry, lay both sheets of vellum over the picture. Staple securely at the top.
3. Practice looking at the picture and then have the "fog" pages obscure the scene.

A TALE FOR EASTER
Paper Daffodils

Supplies:

☐ regular cupcake liners in white

☐ mini cupcake liners in white

☐ yellow and orange markers

☐ spray bottle filled with water

☐ green pipe cleaners

Teacher Guidelines:

1. Beginning with the larger cupcake liner, lay it on the table and flatten it with your palm. Using the markers, scribble on the white liner until it is about half covered with marker. Repeat the flattening and coloring on the mini cupcake liner. Next, spray the liners lightly with water, making the marker colors fade into each other. Let dry.

2. To assemble the flowers, place a mini cupcake liner into the middle of a regular cupcake liner. Scrunch the cupcake liners back into a ruffled edge by twisting the middle of the paper from the back side. Take a green pipe cleaner and wrap one end into a small ball (about ½ inch). Poke the other end through the layered cupcake wrappers and pull until the liners are at the very end of the pipe cleaner and the green ball becomes the center of the flower.

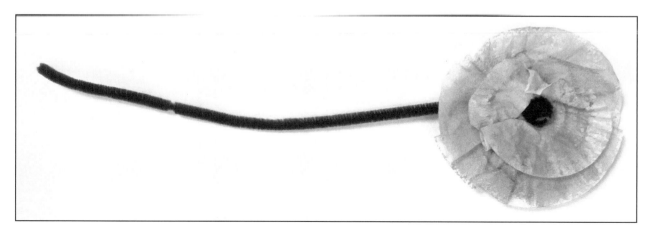

WHAT DO YOU DO WITH A TAIL LIKE THIS?
My Body

Supplies:

- ☐ 4" x 6" picture of your child, filling up the frame from head to foot
- ☐ my body template
- ☐ glue
- ☐ pencil

Teacher Guidelines:

1. Begin by positioning the picture in the center of the template, in the designated "picture" spot. Glue it down to secure it.
2. In the labeled areas, have the child think about the individual body part and why it is important to them. Let them use the pencil to write a one-word answer in the space provided. (i.e., Hands: holding, writing, coloring / Feet: running, walking, jumping)

A HOUSE FOR HERMIT CRAB
Watercolor Crab

Supplies:

- [ ] crab template
- [ ] watercolor paper – 1 piece,
      8.5" x 11" inches
- [ ] watercolor paints

- [ ] paintbrush
- [ ] scissors
- [ ] glue
- [ ] blue piece of construction paper

Teacher Guidelines:

1. Begin by using the watercolor paints and brush to completely fill a piece of watercolor paper with paint. Use as many colors as you want—the more colorful, the better. Set aside to dry.

2. Next, copy the template design onto the watercolor paper by running it through a copy machine. Using the scissors, cut out the crab shapes. On the blue piece of construction paper, shape the crab by placing the watercolored pieces back together in the proper place.

AN EXTRAORDINARY EGG
Salt Texture Egg

Supplies:

- [ ] egg template
- [ ] piece of white cardstock
- [ ] gray and black watercolor paints
- [ ] paintbrush
- [ ] large-grain, coarse salt
- [ ] scissors

Teacher Guidelines:

1. Copy the egg template onto white cardstock paper. With the paintbrush, completely cover the egg with shades of black and gray watercolor paint (a very wet coating works best). While the egg's paint is still wet, sprinkle the salt onto the egg. Let dry.
2. When the egg is dried completely, gently brush off any leftover salt into the trash.
3. To finish, use the scissors to cut out the egg shape.

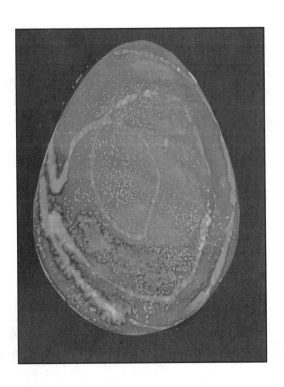

SEVEN SILLY EATERS
Wood Cake Puzzles

Supplies:

- [ ] cake template
- [ ] crayons
- [ ] scissors
- [ ] liquid glue
- [ ] water

- [ ] paintbrush
- [ ] 9 jumbo wooden craft sticks
- [ ] clear tape
- [ ] X-Acto knife (for adult use only)

Teacher Guidelines:

1. Cut the template square from the paper. Using the crayons, color the entire cake shape. Set aside. In a small cup, mix 1 tsp. liquid glue and about 10 drops of water. Stir together with the paintbrush until blended. Next, lay out the jumbo wooden craft sticks so that they line up, flat side touching flat side, in a tight rectangle. Use two 6-inch lengths of clear tape to secure the craft sticks together. Once the sticks are secure, gently flip over the whole set.

2. Next, using the glue and paintbrush, coat each stick (while staying in formation) with a thin layer of the glue, leaving space on the ends (so there won't be excess glue on the parts not covered by the template). Lay the cake picture over the assembled craft sticks and press it firmly into place. Make sure that the cake picture is laying flat on the sticks and that it does not have wrinkles or air bubbles. Set aside to dry for 2 hours.

3. When the picture is dry, have an adult use the X-Acto knife to cut along the seams of each stick (through the paper) to separate the picture. Gently flip over the sticks and remove the tape from the back side. Mix up the sticks and put them back together to make the puzzle.

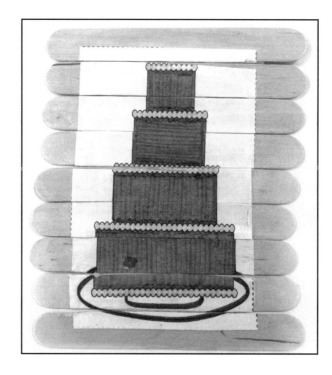

COME ON RAIN
Raindrops

Supplies:

☐ 1 piece of white construction paper   ☐ liquid glue

☐ crayons   ☐ glitter

Teacher Guidelines:

1. Start by drawing a sky scene on the construction paper, including clouds.
2. Drip several small drops of the glue onto the cloud scene.
3. When the scene has several drops of glue, lift the paper from the top and allow the glue to run down the paper, simulating rain. (Be careful of glue dripping off paper.)
4. Sprinkle with glitter.
5. Lay flat to dry.

Literature Crafts

WONDERS OF NATURE
Symmetry Painting

Supplies:

- ☐ butterfly half template
- ☐ 8.5" x 11" white cardstock
- ☐ paints – all colors
- ☐ paintbrush
- ☐ scissors
- ☐ pipe cleaner

Teacher Guidelines:

1. Fold the white cardstock in half along the long edges, creasing the fold well. Open the paper back up and flatten it out. Using the paintbrush, have the child smear paint on one side of the folded paper – not crossing the fold line. Working quickly, while the paint is still wet, fold the paper again along the creased line. Allow the child to smash the folded paper together to make sure that the paint is moved to the blank side of the paper. Open the paper up carefully and set it aside to dry.

2. When the paper is dry, cut out the butterfly half from the template. Lay it gently on the fold of the paper. Cut carefully around the template with the scissors. Unfold. Fold the pipe cleaner in half and wrap it around the small area between the butterfly wings, twisting gently to secure. Curl the ends of the pipe cleaner at the ends to form the antennae.

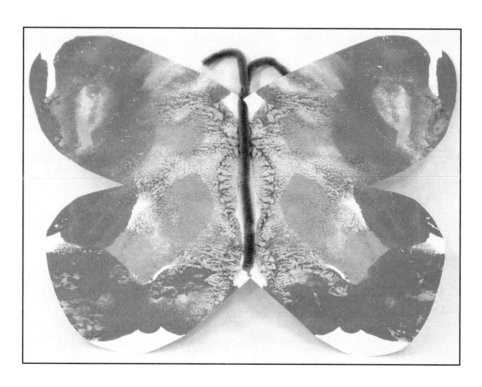

ALL THINGS BRIGHT AND BEAUTIFUL
Nest Building

Supplies:

☐ wax paper

☐ 24 small twigs (about 4 inches long)

☐ white liquid glue

☐ for decoration – small bits of twine, string, moss, greenery, etc.

Teacher Guidelines:

1. Start by laying out a piece of wax paper. Build the first layer of the bird nest by laying out 6 lengths of twig, touching, in a hexagon shape. Squeeze some white glue across the twigs. Let dry.

2. When the base of the nest is dry, begin by placing one row of twigs around the edge of the hexagon shape, overlapping the twig ends with the next one in line. Squeeze some white glue where the twigs touch the base and each other. Set aside to dry.

3. When row one is completely dry, begin creating row two in exactly the same way. Continue row-building until you use all of your twigs, or when the nest is the size you want. You can use twine or moss to decorate your nest.

CONCEPT CRAFTS

PRECISIONISM
Flowers in the Style of Georgia O'Keeffe

Supplies:

☐ small live flower

☐ magnifying glass

☐ notecard

☐ pencil

☐ colored pencils

Teacher Guidelines:

1. Choose a small, live flower to begin. Give the child the magnifying glass and discuss all of the small details that they can see in the flower when they look this closely.
2. Keeping the flower and magnifying glass close for reference, allow the child to loosely sketch what they see in the flower on the notecard. Use the entire front of the notecard to sketch the flower.
3. Use the colored pencils to color the flower as accurately as possible.

Concept Crafts

STILL LIFE WITH APPLES
Apple Prints

Supplies:

- ☐ fresh apples
- ☐ sharp knife (for adult use only)
- ☐ paper towels
- ☐ fork (for adult use only)
- ☐ paper plates
- ☐ paint – yellow, red, and green
- ☐ foam paintbrush
- ☐ white paper or fabric

Teacher Guidelines:

1. To prepare, an adult should cut the apples in half, starting at the stem and down through the bottom.
2. Lay the apples, cut side down, on the paper towels to dry. An adult should stick the fork firmly into the skin side of the apple – this will be the handle for the stamp.
3. Next, squirt a quarter-sized dot of each color of paint onto a different paper plate. Gently press each apple stamp into the paint, swirling it so that the entire cut side of the apple is covered. Stamp onto paper or fabric. Let dry.

POINTILLISM
Painting with Dots

Supplies:

- ☐ flower or any drawn picture template
- ☐ white construction paper
- ☐ paints – various colors
- ☐ cotton swabs

Teacher Guidelines:

1. Begin by transferring the template onto the construction paper.
2. Next, dip the cotton swabs into the paint and begin making small dots on the picture. Change cotton swabs each time you change colors. Fill in the page completely with color and then set aside to dry.

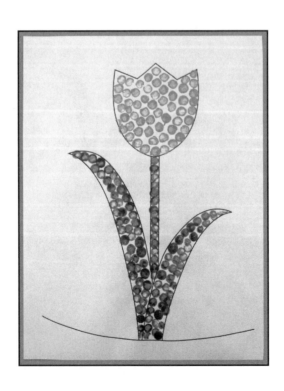

IRISES – VINCENT VAN GOGH
Torn Paper Iris

Supplies:

- [ ] iris template
- [ ] white cardstock
- [ ] construction paper: shades of blues, purples, and greens
- [ ] glue

Teacher Guidelines:

1. Copy the iris template onto the white cardstock.
2. Following Van Gogh's use of color and shades, instruct the child to tear small strips or bits of each color paper and glue them onto the template. Encourage the use of different shades of each color, mimicking Van Gogh's colors.

USING CONSTELLATIONS IN NAVIGATION
(Christopher Columbus)
Creating Orion and Taurus

Supplies:

- [ ] constellations template
- [ ] black construction paper
- [ ] white colored pencil
- [ ] ruler
- [ ] toothpick

Teacher Guidelines:

1. To begin, tape the Orion and Taurus patterns onto the black construction paper.
2. Stressing caution with the toothpick, allow the child to use the toothpick to poke small holes in each of the marked stars. When both constellations are marked, allow the child to use the white pencil and ruler to connect the stars. (Label the constellations with their names if desired.)
3. When finished, have the child stand under a light and hold the black paper up. This should shine light through the poked holes of the paper, illuminating the constellations.

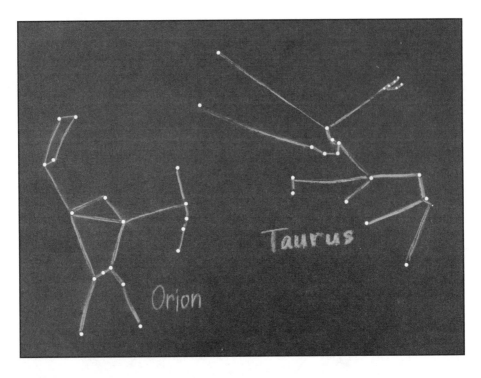

Concept Crafts

MONA LISA – LEONARDO DA VINCI
Self Portraits

Supplies:

☐ hand-held mirror

☐ pencil

☐ 8.5" x 11" white paper

☐ colored pencils

Teacher Guidelines:

1. This craft begins by letting the child study their face in the hand-held mirror. Suggest to the child that they give careful consideration to the shape of their face, their eyes, nose, lips, hair, and any identifying details.

2. Have the child sketch their portrait lightly in pencil, filling in the details with the colored pencils.

STAINED GLASS
Glass Votive Candles

Supplies:

- [ ] small glass votive candle holder (available at any craft store)
- [ ] various colors of tissue paper
- [ ] scissors
- [ ] white liquid glue
- [ ] water
- [ ] bowl
- [ ] paintbrush

Teacher Guidelines:

1. Using the scissors, cut the tissue papers into small shapes. Set aside.
2. In a small bowl, add 3 teaspoons white glue and 1 teaspoon water. Mix together with the paintbrush.
3. Working in small areas, use the paintbrush to apply the glue mixture to the outside of the glass votive holder.
4. When you have a small section covered with glue, apply the small bits of colored tissue paper to the wet glue. Use the paintbrush to make sure the tissue papers are completely attached to the glue and to smooth out any wrinkles in the paper.
5. Continue working in small increments until the entire votive holder is covered.
6. Lastly, apply the remaining bit of glue mixture over the entire surface of the tissue paper. Allow to dry for several hours before adding a candle.

Concept Crafts

WINTER TREES
Creating a Snowy Landscape

Supplies:

- [ ] winter trees template
- [ ] blue cardstock
- [ ] scissors
- [ ] tape
- [ ] white paint
- [ ] water
- [ ] old toothbrush

Teacher Guidelines:

1. Using the scissors, cut out the winter scene from the template. Discard the tree shapes, saving only the negative space around the trees.
2. Carefully line up the cut negative space to the top edge of the cardstock (horizontal). Use a small amount of tape to secure the template to the page.
3. Next, thin the white paint using a small amount of water. Dip the toothbrush into the thinned paint and tap off any excess. Hold the brush over the paper, bristles side down, and gently fan the toothbrush bristles with your thumb. This will splatter the paint onto the cardstock, making snow-covered tree shapes. Add as much "snow" to the picture as you want. When you are finished, set aside to dry.
4. Remove the taped template when the picture is completely dry.

STARRY NIGHT – VINCENT VAN GOGH
Shaving Cream Painting

Supplies:

- ☐ Starry Night sky template
- ☐ white cardstock
- ☐ 9" x 13" inch pan
- ☐ shaving cream
- ☐ acrylic paints – blues, purples, and yellows
- ☐ popsicle stick
- ☐ plastic ruler

Teacher Guidelines:

1. Copy the Starry Night template onto the cardstock. Set aside.
2. Squirt shaving cream into the bottom of the pan, enough to cover the bottom. Spread the shaving cream around, making the surface as smooth as possible.
3. Next, drop large lines of acrylic paint into the shaving cream, keeping in mind the locations of the colors in Van Gogh's painting.
4. With the popsicle stick, swirl the paints into the shaving cream, trying to copy the lines in the Starry Night painting. When the colors are where you would like them, drop the template page into the shaving cream mixture—face down. Press the paper gently into the mixture and let it sit for 30 seconds. Remove the paper by lifting it straight up. Set it aside, paint side up, for 5 minutes.
5. After sitting for the 5 minutes, use the ruler to gently squeegee the shaving cream from the paper. Set aside to dry completely.

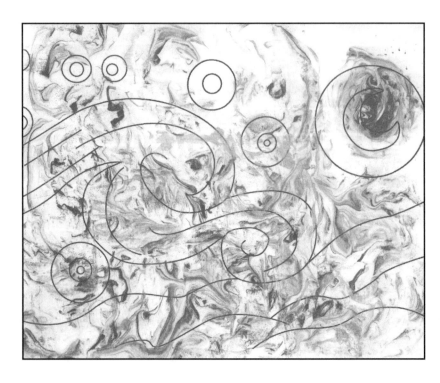

SUNFLOWERS – VINCENT VAN GOGH
Sunflower Pastels

Supplies:

- ☐ circles template
- ☐ scissors
- ☐ masking tape
- ☐ white construction paper
- ☐ art pastels – yellows, browns, and greens

Teacher Guidelines:

1. Begin by cutting out the circles from the template, using the scissors.
2. Taking a length of masking tape, circle it back around on itself so that it forms a loop. Attach the tape to the back of a circle and place it on the white construction paper. Repeat for all circles. Holding the circles in place with one hand, use the other hand to make small yellow stripes that begin on the inner edge of the circle and move out about 2 inches.
3. When the circles have all been striped, use a finger to gently smudge the yellow stripes into sunflower leaves. Remove the circles.
4. Next, make a small pattern of dots inside where the circle templates were and use a finger to smudge the insides of the sunflower. Continue coloring and smudging the sunflowers by adding detail and leaves.

SNOWFLAKES
Salt Crystal Snowflakes

Supplies:

☐ blue construction paper   ☐ coarse salt

☐ white glue

Teacher Guidelines:

1. Using the glue, draw simple snowflake shapes on the construction paper.
2. Moving quickly, sprinkle coarse salt onto the glue snowflakes.
3. Shake off excess salt.
4. Set aside to dry.

Concept Crafts

UNITED STATES OF AMERICA
Torn Paper Flag

Supplies:

☐ 2 pieces white construction paper
☐ pencil
☐ red construction paper
☐ blue construction paper
☐ glue

Teacher Guidelines:

1. Begin by looking at the U.S. flag, or a picture of one. Using the pencil, roughly sketch out the blue section of the flag in the upper left corner (landscape) of the white construction paper.
2. Next, tear thin strips of red construction paper (the long way). Glue those red strips down to the paper, leaving white space between each stripe. This will be the alternating white stripes on the flag.
3. Next, fill in the roughed-in rectangle that was outlined in pencil with blue construction paper. Secure with glue.
4. Lastly, tear very small bits of white paper construction paper for the flag's stars. Secure the "stars" to the blue area with glue. Set aside to dry completely.

EASTER CROSS
Tissue Paper Cross

Supplies:

☐ clear packing tape

☐ scissors

☐ pen

☐ tissue paper (many colors cut into 1-inch squares)

Teacher Guidelines:

1. Cut one strip of packing tape 18 inches long with scissors. Place on a flat surface, sticky side up.
2. With the pen, mark the tape at 9 inches (the halfway point on the tape).
3. Place cut tissue paper squares onto the sticky side of the tape from the marked middle point to the cut edge. Try not to overlap the squares, but do not worry if the squares hang off the edge of the tape (we will trim them at the end). Fill in the entire half.
4. Working from the side without the tissue paper, carefully fold the tape strip in half, making sure the edges of the tape match up and that the tape has no bubbles or wrinkles. Press firmly to secure.
5. Cut another strip of packing tape 8 inches long. Place on a flat surface, sticky side up.
6. Mark the tape at 4 inches (the halfway point on the tape).
7. Center the completed 9-inch tape strip on one of the half portions of tape. The completed strip should be centered in the 4-inch half with about 2 inches hanging over the top. This will be the vertical bar on the cross.
8. Working in the same half that the completed strip is in, fill in any portions of tape that are not covered by the completed strip with tissue. Do not put any tissue paper over the completed strip area.
9. Fold the smaller tape strip at the halfway mark and press it firmly into place.
10. Trim any tissue paper that hangs over the tape.

NATURAL BIRD FEEDER

Supplies:

☐ toilet paper roll

☐ plastic spoon

☐ solid shortening (at room temperature)

☐ small plate

☐ bird seed

Teacher Guidelines:

1. Slide the toilet paper roll onto two spread fingers to hold it. Using the spoon, spread a thin (1/8-1/4 inch) layer of shortening onto the entire outside of the roll.

2. Pour the bird seed onto the plate. Gently roll the shortening-covered roll in the bird seed, pressing down slightly so that the seed adheres to the roll. Shake off excess seed back onto the plate and set aside to firm up for about 10 minutes.

3. When ready, slip the bird feeder roll onto a small tree limb for the birds to enjoy.

TEMPLATES

PASSPORT

*United States
of America*

PASSPORT

*United States
of America*

Name:

Picture

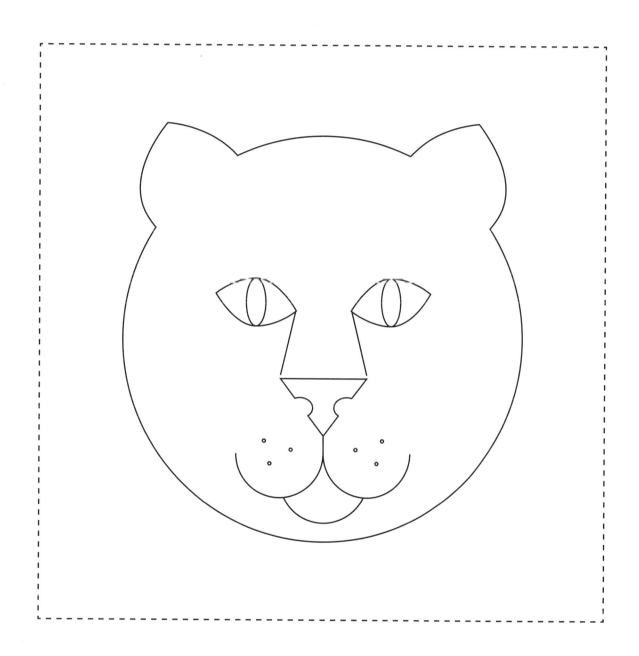

The Important
Thing About Blue:

The Important
Thing About Red:

Name
_____

The Important
Thing About Green:

My
Important
Book

The Important
Thing About Yellow:

The Important
Thing About Me:

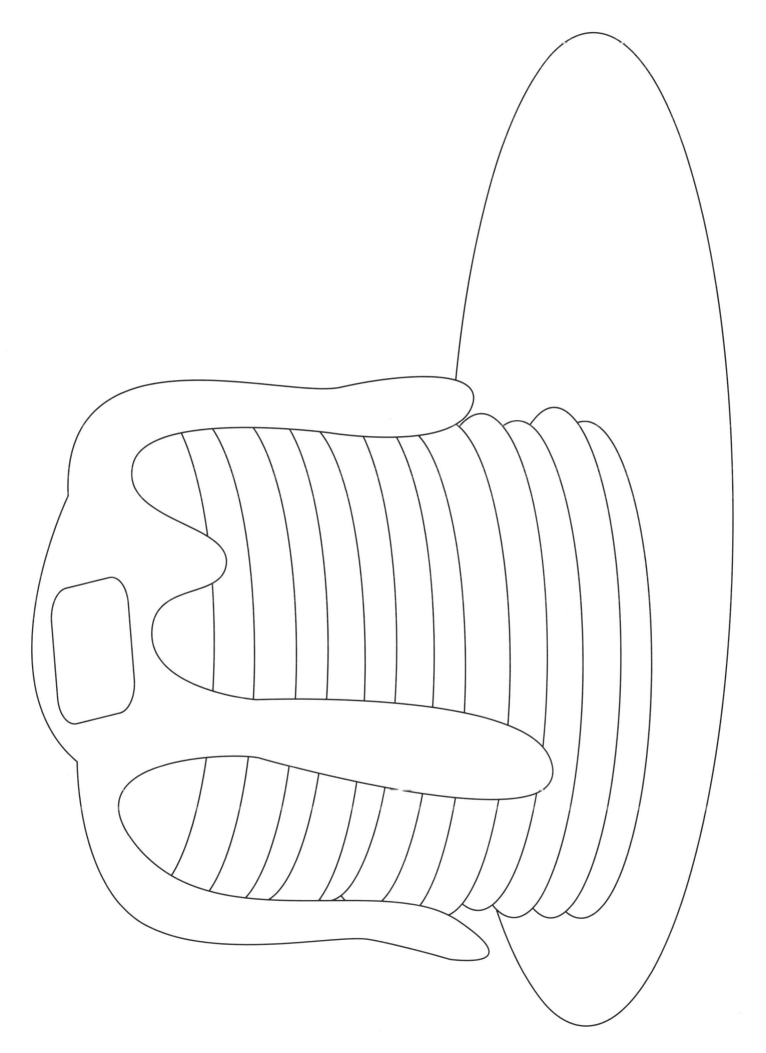

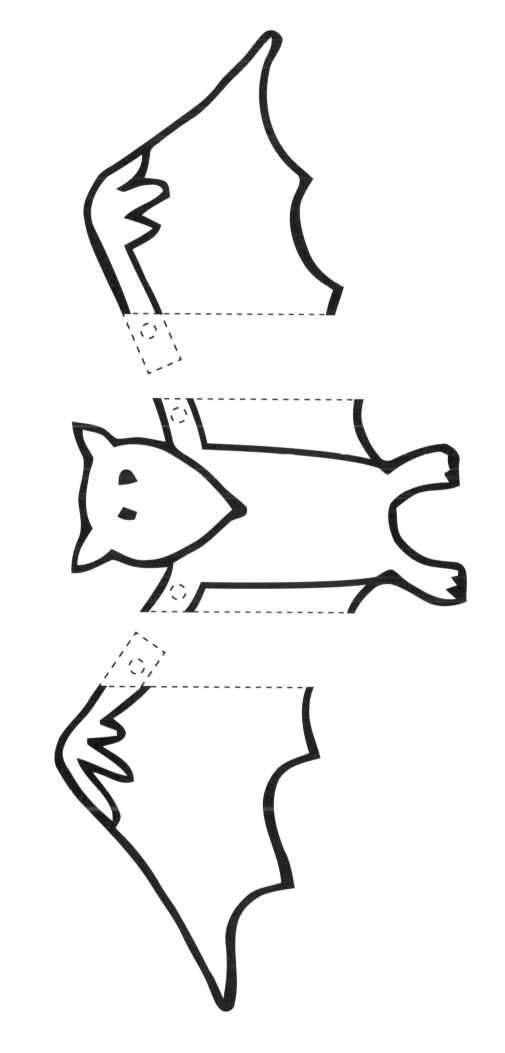

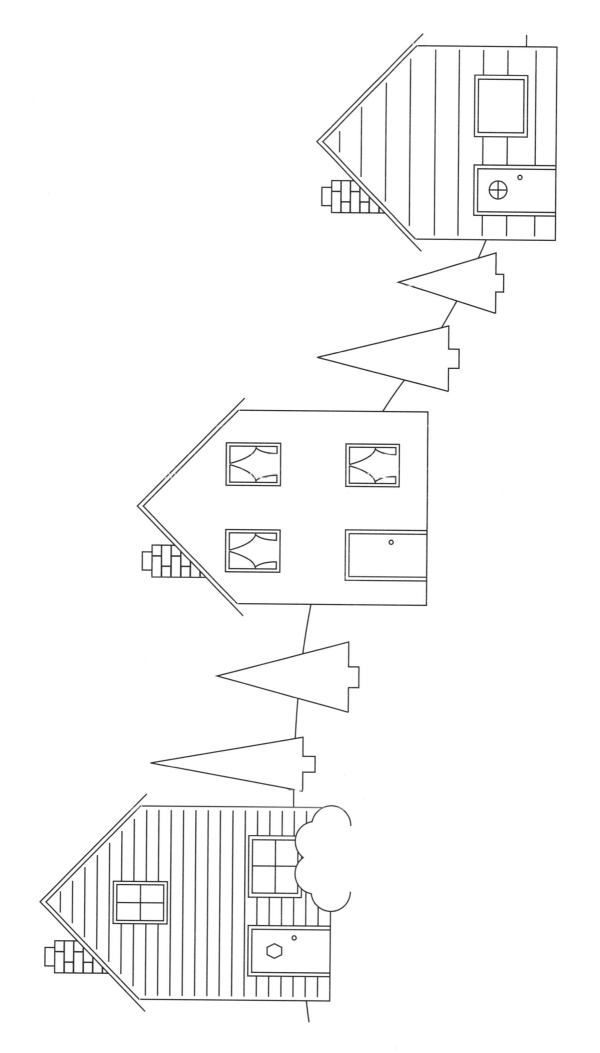

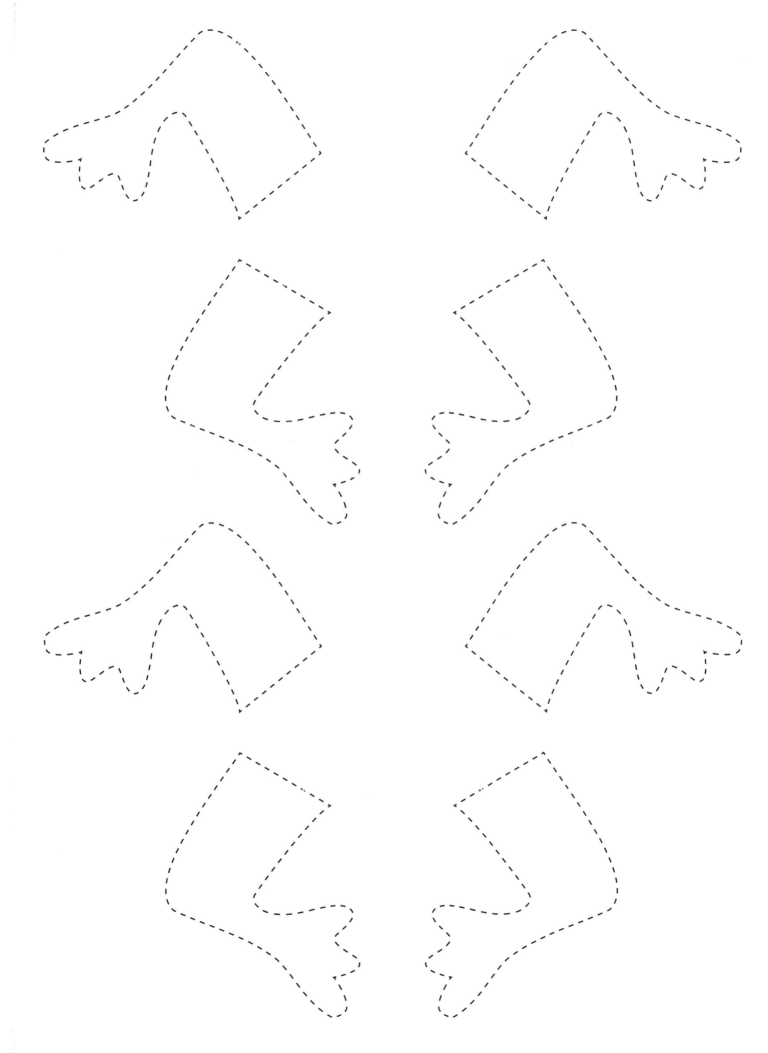

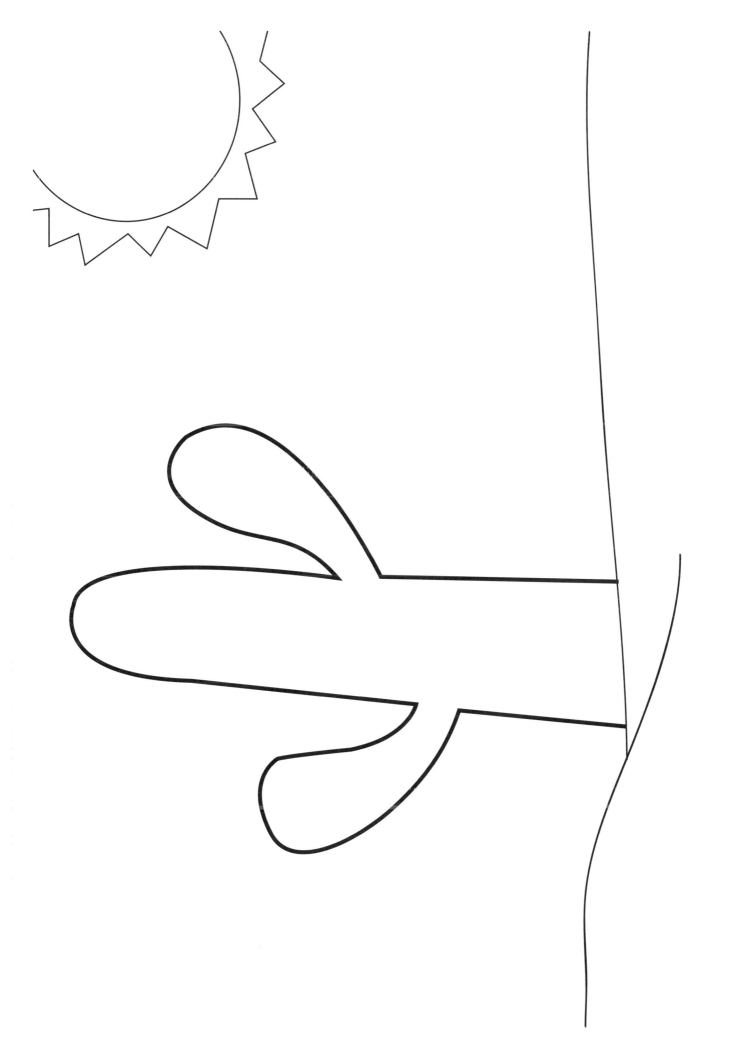

Hair

_____

Eyes

_____

Nose

_____

Ears

_____

Arm

_____

Picture Here

Hands

_____

Legs

_____

Feet

_____

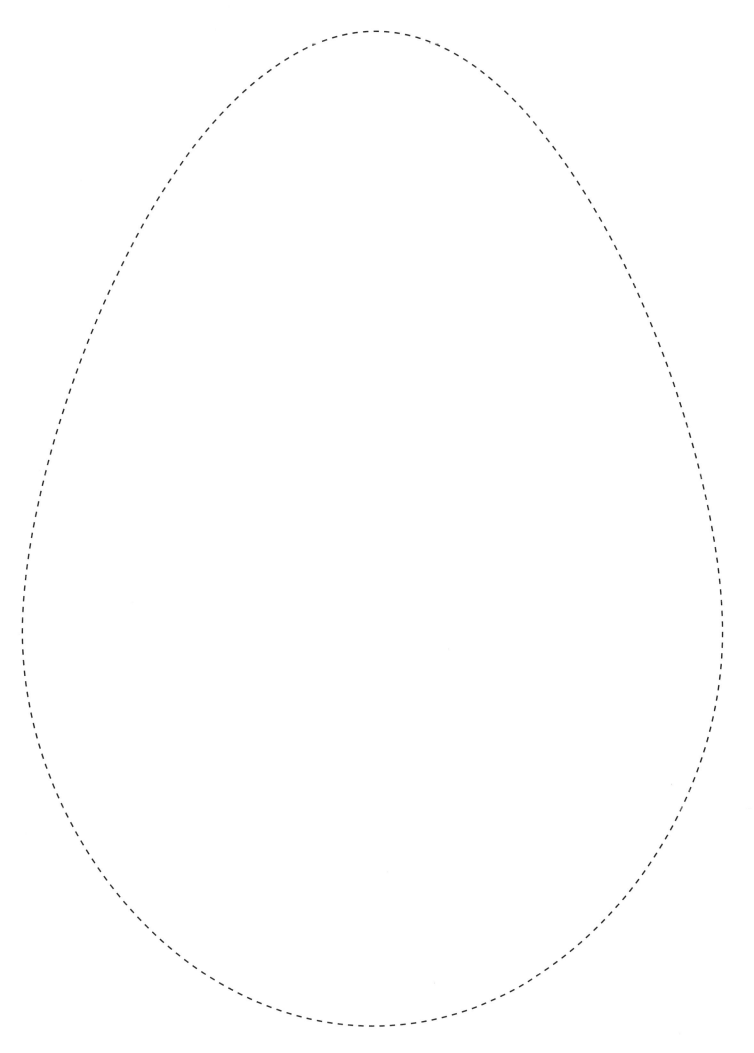

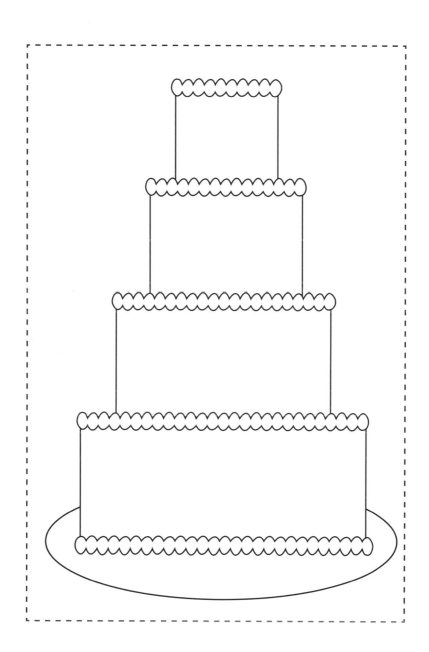

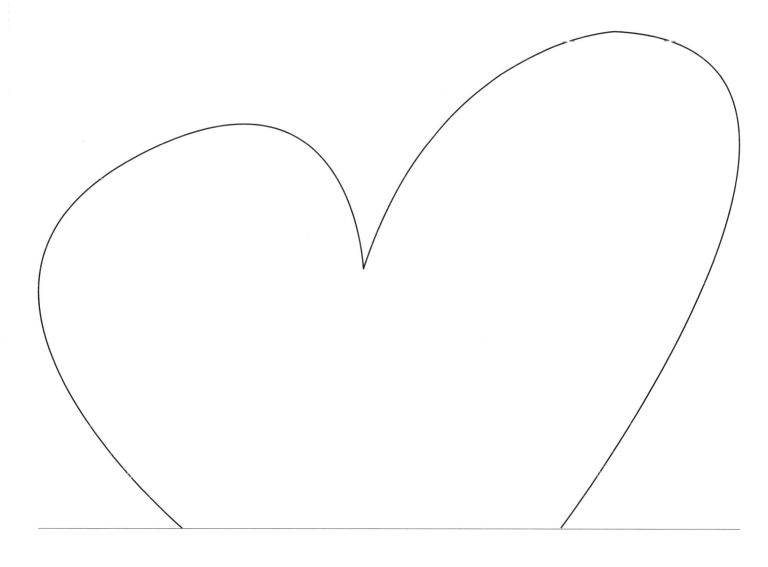

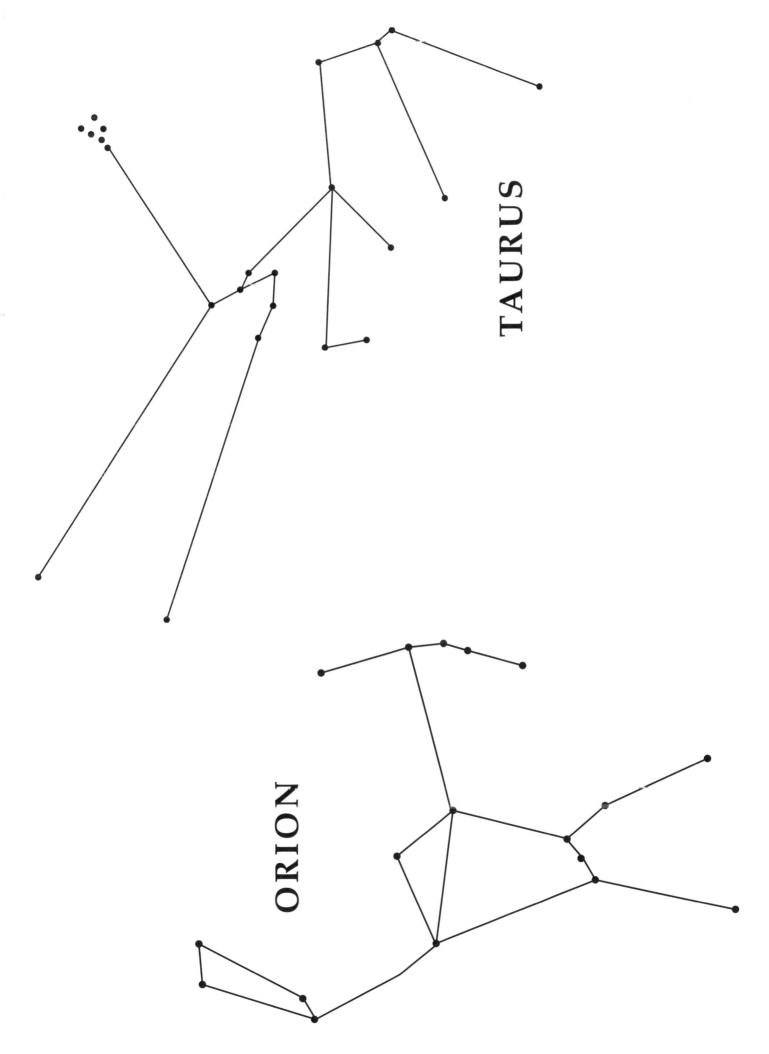